Pet Loss Poems

To Heal Your Heart and Soul

Wendy Van de Poll MS, CEOL

Spirit Paw Press, LLC
Concord, New Hampshire, USA

Pet Loss Poems
To Heal Your Heart and Soul

Copyright 2018 Spirit Paw Press, LLC
Wendy Van de Poll, MS, CEOL

Published by Spirit Paw Press, LLC, Concord, NH 03303

Cover design: Danijela Mijailovic
Page layout & pre-press: Lighthouse24

Publisher's Cataloging-in-Publication Data
provided by Five Rainbows Cataloging Services

Names: Van de Poll, Wendy, author.
Title: Pet loss poems : to heal your heart and soul / Wendy Van de Poll, MS, CEOL.
Description: Concord, NH : Center for Pet Loss Grief, 2018. | Series: Pet loss poem series, bk. 1.
Identifiers: ISBN 978-1-7324375-2-4 (softcover)
Subjects: LCSH: Pets--Death--Psychological aspects. | Pet owners--Psychology. | Loss (Psychology) | Pet loss--Poetry. | Poetry--Collections. | BISAC: POETRY / Subjects & Themes / Death, Grief, Loss. | POETRY / American / General.
Classification: LCC PS3622.A585361 P48 2018 (print) | LCC PS3622.A585361 (ebook) | DDC 811/.6--dc23.

Disclaimer

Although the author and publisher have made every effort to ensure that the information in this book was correct at the time of publishing, the author and publisher do not assume and hereby disclaim any liability to any party for any loss, damage, or disruption caused by errors or omissions, whether such errors or omissions result from negligence, accident, or other cause.

If you ever feel like you can no longer function with your life, become suicidal, and find that normal grief feelings have become extremely difficult for you to bear, then that is considered unhealthy grief. This is the time to call your hospital, medical practitioner psychologist, or other health care provider who is trained to help you.

Do not isolate yourself if you are experiencing unhealthy grief. Get the professional help you require.

Thank You!

Thank you for purchasing *Pet Loss Poems: To Heal Your Heart and Soul.* To show my appreciation, I am offering personalized pet loss poems for my readers.

Please visit:
https://centerforpetlossgrief.com/personalized-pet-loss-poem

To all the animals
who grace our lives and
help us be better humans.

Contents

Introduction

Is your heart raw from the loss of your pet? Are you struggling to find peace in the daily routine that you once shared with your beloved companion?

In this book I am sharing with you forty-one pet loss grief poems I wrote to help my clients heal their grief and find solace on a daily basis.

Writing them also helped me process my grief and heal while helping my clients with their journey.

These poems are individually distinctive, empathetic, and honest. They express many emotions that normally accompany the loss of a pet as well as the passage through grief that people experience. As you read these poems, my hope is you will be able to find peace, joy, and compassion, healing your heart as you experience the stories these poems tell.

In this poetry book you will find familiarity, reverence, solemnity, kindheartedness, and even moments of humor. You will experience intimate details of the varying types of relationships people have with their animals.

It is my hope that this book of poems will contribute to your healing journey by providing you with a compassionate path others have taken.

Pet Loss Poems: To Heal Your Heart and Soul was written because people who suffer pet loss grief need a soft place to land. We need a place where our minds can take a break—an accommodation to spark our imagination for hope as we process our emotions. Many have found that this book of poetry offers many kind words for healing.

With this book, I am offering a special opportunity for you to have your own *Personalized Pet Loss Poem*. The link for this service can be found in the Resource Section in the back of this book.

With years of experience in supporting people as their pets reach the end of their lives, I have gained much wisdom and knowledge concerning the souls of our beloved companions.

Our animals are incredibly generous and have a unique view of the world and of us. They come into our lives for many reasons—each one personal. They have a profound effect on us and on the way we approach life.

Both personal and professional experience have equipped me to help countless people around the world feel safe with expressing their feelings of grief; my poems and I provide a compassionate outlet to express what they are feeling. I have been a professional animal communicator for over 20 years and a certified end-of-life and pet loss grief coach (CEOL); I have also served as a licensed massage therapist for humans, horses, and hounds, and I am a wolf biologist, as well.

People who feel alone in their feelings of grief have found support with these poems. Many have shared with me that reading this book has helped them feel sustained as they follow their daily routine.

Isabel, for whom I wrote the personalized poem, "How Could I Forget?" (p. 30), shared:

Wendy,

Thank you for my beautiful poem about Dandy and including it in this book. I love my poem and reading what others are experiencing. This book is something I really needed as I was going through such a difficult time. When I read a particular poem on a daily basis I find that I can focus my thoughts through the love that is shared. It helps me not to feel alone in this journey. This is such a difficult subject, but the poems are compassionate, honest, and good for the heart and soul. One of the toughest things about saying good-bye to Dandy was knowing I would never hold him in my arms again. These poems helped me understand there are other ways to feel his love and companionship. Thank you for opening up my heart and mind to feel the creative part of my emotional grieving.

When you read this book, you are entering a heartfelt and creative place which has healed many a grieving heart. I assure you that, when you read these poems, you will experience relief that others have felt, others who have felt grief similar to what you are going through.

You never have to feel alone in your pet loss grief!

Remember, there are many ways to walk the journey of pet loss grief. My other books address this topic in great detail. By experiencing the Pet Loss Poems in this book, I hope you will allow your creative side to take a heartfelt journey towards feeling blessed and thankful for the life you shared with your beloved companion.

Respectfully,

Wendy Van de Poll

July 23, 2018

So Fast

So many days spent on the porch,
Your friendly growl igniting the torch
And keeping all the cats away.
How the sun keeps it dry on a rainy day.

I feel your heart
Beating so fast;
You small tiny thing
Your life moves so fast.

Sometimes I wish
We could pace it the same:
When I go, you go;
I stay, you remain.

I'd stare dumbfounded
At how precious a face
You'd look at me with,
When we cozily embraced.

Cuddles and snuggles
That left long ago;
Now I just remember
When you'd catch, and I'd throw.

Friendship

Don't try to tell me
He's just a pet;
You don't know him like I do.
He's more than a friend.

He listens,
He cuddles,
He doesn't keep score.

And best of all,
Lately,
Stopped scratching the door.

I trust him completely.
'Twas never a doubt;
And I love when he greets me
Day in and day out.

I'll always remember
Those days sitting still,
When his thoughts and my thoughts
Shared the ink from the quill.

November

Amber-sweet petals
Fall at your feet
As you trot ahead of me
To your own inner beat.

We sample the weather
All the year round
But in fall, on the sidewalk
Is where we're always found.

You must know you're my favorite
Without any doubt;
I'd give up whatever
Just to snuggle your snout.

I Never Wanted You

I never wanted you.
I said we should get a poodle
Or perhaps a cat.

But you wandered, uninvited,
Through an open back gate into our lives.

The kids threw their arms around you.
A long, dangling ribbon of drool fell into
    my daughter's hair.
Your whip-like tail raised welts on my wife's legs.
"This dog?" I asked.

I thought I might be saved by whomever had lost you
But there was no reply to the ads and posters and—

After years of drool plastered on the glass doors
Where you watched for us to come home each day,
Pounding paws, joyful sloppy greetings,

All knick-knacks removed from low tables
To protect them from your always-happy whiptail—

I think to myself, you were never lost.
You found us because you were the dog we needed
To bring happy chaos into an overly-ordered life.

On the day you leave your body
Lying on your favorite rug,
I imagine you'll wander, invited,
    into the gate of heaven,
There to make a wonderful, happy nuisance
    of yourself with the angels.
I wish I could be like my dog.

Innocent Smile

I never wanted
To say goodbye;
I remember how much
You'd hate it when I cry.

But, Love, I can't help it;
Now that you're not here,
I need to release
This new buildup of fear.

Without your sweet nothings
Nibbled on my ear,
I'm afraid I feel lonely
And must shed just one tear

In memory of you,
Of your innocent smile.
I start to feel better;
The tears rest for a while.

But still I'm not happy
Without your sweet face;
The memories beguile me,
Lost without a trace.

The Chase

Hey, Big Eyes,
I've got a surprise.

Heck yes, it's a string
With a bell on the end.

You, ready to pounce,
Eyes now more pronounced,

Focused in stare
On the treasure I bear.

If I could do anything,
I'd freeze your cute face,

Focused forever
On playing the chase.

Your soft, dewy features,
Calling to my heart,

Where I'll love you forever,
You sweet work of art.

I Wish I Could Live Like My Dog

Ask "Why not?" instead of "What for?"
Try before wondering if I can.
Never quit before I begin.

Neither ask for permission
Nor give apologies,
But still sometimes have the dignity
To look ashamed when I've ruined something.

Splash in life's mud puddles,
Relish a joy, run through an open door.
I Wish I Could Live Like My Dog.

Roll in what delights me—
Even if others think it's stinky.

Chase what moves,
Live with indifference to the rules.
Love completely and express it often;
Live as if life is short and good.

Go to sleep when the time is right.
I Wish I Could Live Like My Dog!

Lucky

Tenderly batting
Your paws through my hair,
Your eyes whisper sweet nothings,
Floating love through the air.

My Sweet, I'm surrounded
By your soulful heart;
I don't even mind it
When you softly fart.

No matter how smelly
Your breath may well be.
I lap it like brandy;
It's whiskey to me.

Now that you're gone,
I can still smell your fur
And remember the softness
As I stroked while you purred.

You'll never be forgotten
As long as I find
Your hair on my clothes
And your meow in my mind.

Treats and Soft Kisses

It really doesn't matter
Whether dog, cat or salamander,
They hold a special power,
For your sadness they devour.

Kitten scratches and dog bites,
Balls of string and big appetites,
Bones chewed and balls thrown:
Just some of the things that you have now known.

They pull you in with a delicate gaze,
Light up your life, leaving your heart ablaze,
Never asking for much except that you appear
With treats and soft kisses whenever you're near.

Meaning everything to you
    with only a glance,
You know they're meant for you
    'cause nothing's by chance.
You'll give them what you have
    no matter how much;
All you ask in return
    is for their loving touch.

When they leave you after that final caress,
They mean no harm nor any undue duress;
For loving you completely with all of their heart
Is what they had in mind for you right from the start.

Though now they are gone
    and away from your sight,
You can still feel their gaze
    and you know it is right
That they've left you only for a while
    and not really for good,
For they still think of you as only
    a soul companion would.

Companionship

Softly snuggled into my side
Whether working or playing
Or out for a ride,

You're my first companion
And all bets aside,
I'd safely say you're my "ride or die."

I love when you nibble
Your teeth on my toes;
How much you do love me always shows.

I'll love you forever
No matter my woes,
Never forgetting your soft, wet little nose.

It's Only Exciting When You Can't Reach

We both liked to run better than walk and
Throw ourselves into the waves.
Her with ready wagging tail,
    me anxious about leaving the beach.
She laughed at me—
    it's only exciting when you can't reach.

I was the worrier
Wondering if we were pushing our bounds.
She never knew any limit.
She was the last to notice when she slowed down.

What will I do without my dog?
I worry, agonize about what to say,
What to do, how to let go.
As usual, she shows me the way.

Life is short, she tells me with calm eyes;
Don't be afraid of what you don't know.
It won't make it safer to go slow;
It's only exciting when you can't reach.

Pitter Patter

Deep in midwinter
I struggled to find
A friend who could leave me
Feeling truly sublime.

But then I heard something
That startled me straight,
A slight pitter-patter
From outside my gate.

I shot to the window
Like some kind of snoop
Only to find there
A dog on my stoop.

He looked kind of ragged,
As though he was wild;
However, for me,
He became like a child.

I loved him through seasons
From sunshine to snow;
We shared some good memories
As I watched him grow.

And now as he leaves me,
The gifts he'll bestow
Are the winters he loved me
And kept my heart aglow.

Always in My Heart

Although I will miss you
And some days will be hard,
I know I can't keep you
For your soul must embark.
You've done so much good
With the time you were given
And I consider myself lucky
To have been your special human.
Even though you're no longer here,
We will never be far apart,
For I will hold you forever
Always, in my heart.

My Dog's Job

Some dogs protect, some dogs hunt,
Other dogs are soldiers, bomb squad and cop.
Dogs are rescuers and workers in hard labor—
And then there is my dog,
Whose job is humor.

A silly, simple job you might think.
With her underbite and mismatched ears, frizzled hair
Standing up everywhere, it should be easy.
And nature did, I don't deny, well equip my dog for
    her career.

But some days are hard.
Some days are sad, lonely and long.
And the last thing I want is to laugh.

But my little dog—
She does her job well
With a routine so hilarious it brings me to tears:
Jumping about and squeaky toy props
And a wagging tail on an upward-pointed rump.

And on those hard days
When I come home after my dog has gone,
I remember hers was the most important
Of all the dog jobs in the world.

How Could I Forget?
for Isabel and Dandy

How could I forget
The day I took you home,
Your eyes filled with love
As if you knew me all along?
I never knew I needed you
Until you needed me.
I like to think I rescued you,
But you did the rescuing.
There was never a bad day
With you by my side;
Your wet-nose kisses
Soon became my guide.
As you grew throughout the years,
So did my heart.
I loved you more each minute;
I loved you from the start.
I knew the time would come
When I'd have to say goodbye,
But the time we were given
Changed my entire life.
How could I forget
The day you went home,
Your eyes filled with memories
As your soul drifted on?

I Am Not Gone

You can find me in the gentle breeze,
In the sunlight dancing through the trees.
You can find me in the quiet rain;
In the rivers and oceans, I remain.
You can find me when you look inside;
Within your heart is where I reside.
I will never leave; I am not gone.
I'm still here;
I just moved on.

I'll Never Be Far Away

Do you remember when you first took me in?
We did not know each other,
But I knew we would be friends.
Do you remember when I'd sleep on your lap?
I liked your cuddles the most;
We shared the best naps.
Do you remember when I'd *purr* out of the blue?
You may not know this,
But that's how I'd say, "I love you."
Do you remember when I'd bathe in the sunlight?
Our home always felt warm;
Every little thing was alright.
Do you remember all my happy days?
Hold onto those memories,
And I'll never be far away.

She'll Be Back Tomorrow

The dog lies on a pile of her dirty clothes,
Her shoes, a jacket that slipped from where
She'd hung it carelessly as she left.
Only with his face buried in her scent will he rest.

I wonder, as he nibbles
    without interest at his food,
If, when the scent of her fades,
    he might forget,
If the passing of years
    would take away the sting.
If the dog, like a jilted lover,
    might recover and find another.

I drag him out for a walk,
Bribed unsuccessfully with treats and tennis ball,
Reluctant to leave a pair of her socks.
If only I could tell him:
She'll be back tomorrow.

My Promise

You will be with me always,
In my heart and in my mind.
If ever I hear a sad meow,
I'll remember to be kind.

When there comes a time
To save another kitty's life,
I will do so willingly,
With your spirit in mind.

For even though you are gone,
I will help you to live on
By sharing the love you gave me
And passing it on.

This Silence

This silence is not eased by radio or TV
Or even the chatter of friends and family.
It is the clatter of paws, a whine at the door,
A bark, a playful growl, a squeaky-toy squeak,
Gone from the house these years.

"Get a puppy!" my daughter says, "Get another Lab!"
Another Lab! As if this silence were
Like a broken speaker...go buy another.

My sneaky daughter said,
"Pick up some cat food on the way over."
Rows of cages, a sign that says, "Adopt."
No, I think, trying not to look.

But he is looking at me.
He whines and his soft eyes offer to fill this silence.
Where did this leash come from?
This bowl, this bed, this toy,
This sweet companion by my side?

I thank my sneaky daughter
For the noise that again fills my life.

A Purr-fect Escape

You've never ventured out
Beyond the yard
And Sunday was not the time;
I couldn't wait
To see you again
So our hearts could intertwine.

But when I returned
And found you gone,
I knew you had strayed too far.
Your cat bowl was full,
Your mice in a row,
Yet the door was slightly ajar.

It perplexes me; I need to know
Why you would leave
And stray so far from home;
Yet here I sit by the door,
One week since you left
Feeling utterly and completely alone.

I wish I could hear
That simple meow
Upon the doorstep now,
Yet silence persists
As my mind resists
To send you my final vow—

I will watch for you here
And keep your bed warm
For your spirit to come and go.
Though you may never return,
I held you once, and
Your love I'll always know!

When Important Tasks Are Forgotten

Ironclad, my resolve
To finish this project—some hugely important task
I don't remember now—
And my dog came pestering me to play.
So important (this forgotten project)
    that I shooed her away.

On I worked with unwavering determination
But my little dog would not be dissuaded.
She chewed on my toes and pounced on my feet
And dropped no fewer than three toys around me
Until, with persistent barks, she drew me from my task

Out into the sunshine for a game of fetch,
A cardinal singing from an orange tree in bloom,
Mist steaming from damp grass,
And some secret satisfaction in my little dog's smile,
Having reminded me what life is about
When important tasks are forgotten.

Thank you for pestering,
For pouncing,
For chewing,
For smiling, and
For reminding me to forget the lesser things!

Purpose

Dogs come into this world
And give it hope.
They enter our homes
And give them soul.
They devote their lives
And make us whole.
That is their purpose:
To teach us to live,
To laugh,
To love.

When dogs leave this world,
We must not lose their hope,
Their soul,
Their purpose;
As teachers they expect us
To have faith,
To continue to live,
To laugh,
And to love.

Until I Knew a Cat

I never knew love
until I knew a cat
who came into my life,
waiting on my doormat.

I didn't need a pet;
I had a lot going on.
But as fate would have it,
this cat needed a home.

So I gave it a shot
And let this kitty in.
Little did I know,
my life was about to begin.

Who would have known,
a cat could open my eyes
to what it means to love,
without an end in sight?

Even though I miss you
and you are no longer here,
I still feel you close;
in my heart you are near.

I never knew love
until I knew a cat.

Remember

Remember me in my youth,
Full of energy and light,
How we'd sit in the grass,
Watching the birds take flight.

Remember my unconditional love;
If you were sad, I'd cheer you up
And I'll never forget your kisses
Or your amazing belly rubs.

Remember the bond between us,
The quiet understanding we shared.
You were my forever companion;
Nothing else can ever compare.

Remember all the good times I had;
The life you gave me was the best.
Thank you for loving me;
Now I can peacefully rest.

When I Am Gone

When I am gone
Think of me;
If you are sad,
Try not to be.
This is not goodbye,
For I am not gone;
This is not the end,
For in your heart
I live on.

Dog Days

I long for your lick of love,
Wet nose upon my cheek,
Hot, panting breath of affection.
I shall miss you always,
My companion of forever.
Time too short,
Unforgotten memories
Of your paws in my life!

The Cat's Meow

At first I came running to
Your plaintive weep
When seeing my warmth and tenderness
Even as you sleep;
For your kitten's refrain
Formed a connection so deep,
It has sealed my bond to you:
A promise I shall evermore keep.

Then, as you stood
    in our kitchen and yowled,
You savored your food,
    whether fish, fur or fowl.
I promised to feed you
    and made a solemn vow
That nothing would harm you,
    neither dog, hawk, nor owl.

Yet your meows got more direct
    as the years passed by;
They told of your ailments
    and the symptoms that were nigh.
I did my best to soothe you
    and put a twinkle back in your eye,
But, alas! You stole away from me
    with naught but a tiny sigh.

Though I weep for you daily
    and miss your kitty ways,
I know you are happy
    and living in a better place;
And while I long for your gentle purrs
    and touch of moistened nose,
I'm satisfied knowing
    we once were very close.

A Pain So Great

I knew it would be hard,
But this hard?
You have loved me all your life
Unconditionally,
A model of love in perfection;
I miss you so much.
The pain,
Sometimes almost too great,
Reflects what we had,
What we shared,
What we will always know
In mind and spirit
Forever.

My Witness

I held you in my arms
As you passed over,
The veil so thin sometimes;
I can almost touch you still—
The smell of your fur is
The same,
The softness of your body is
The same,
The willingness to be stroked and loved is
The same—yet different.
I am but my own witness now
To your love, to your receiving;
And being it,
I shall always remember
What we had together!

Come into My Arms

Come into my arms,
My loved one.
Let me nestle you one more time,
For ours is a bond
So great
It will never perish.
Ours is a love so deep
It will never be forgotten.
Ours is a union so complete
It will let our spirits fly far,
And sing and dance in the heavens
Together forever more!

A Purr-fect Union

We have walked together
For days on end,
Loved each other
Deeply until
The you in me
Was no different than
The me in you.
Traveling in tandem,
We have crossed many miles,
Shared many times,
Brought many smiles,
And purred together
In the deep, sweet softness
Of our cuddling caress—
I honor whom we have been together.

Sweet Kindness

Your eyes said it all;
So deep yet so small,
One look is all I needed
To know how you were,
What you were thinking.
How close you watched whatever I did.
You protected me,
And warmed my heart;
You respected me
From the very start.
You honored me,
As I do you
Forever and always—
May our paths cross again!

An Ocean So Deep

Your love filled the spaces
    between our touch;
Your kindness poured over me
    with every passing brush.
I have never known a being
    I cared for so much;
The void of your passing
    has silenced that hush.

I think of you now
    as I drift off to sleep;
There were so many promises
    I said I would keep.
For one, I would have snuggled you
    when the night was still deep;
And two, I'd have comforted you
    when some loss made you weep.

But now it's my turn to return what you gave
And send you off to your temporary grave
And guard you
And protect you
And let your spirit soar on love's ocean wave!

For Want of More Love

You left me there,
Crying,
The cold walls of the hospital
Laid bare
Like my soul,
Not believing
You were gone—
A breath, one sigh away
From feeling you in my arms.
I can barely believe
You are gone.
My mind reels in shock,
My heart in sadness;
My body aches inside, knowing
You will be gone tomorrow
And again the next day
And the next day after that.
I miss you and long to hold you deeply.

The Miracle of Your Love

You asked for nothing,
You took nothing,
You lacked nothing.
So remarkable,
A being like yours,
Near perfection it would seem,
Has taken on a new meaning
In life,
As in death,
A boundless compassion,
A fathomless amount of love
You have graced me with
All these years.
You have made me who I am,
A more whole spirit,
A more loving human being.
Thank you!

How Could You Do This Now?

Your unending joy
Permeates my life.
Unbridled compassion,
Unconditional love,
Sloppy wet kisses
Below and above:
There isn't one thing I would change about you!

Ok, maybe one.
Could you live a little longer, please?
It's just not fair.
We have nestled and nurtured each other
All of these years,
Yet all that will be left are memories
And little bits of your tender hair.

How could you do this to me,
Deciding to leave me now?
I'm just not ready to have you go
And I'm unwilling to just make it somehow!

I feel you slipping away too fast
Yet there's nothing I can do
Except pray that your transition
Is peaceful and kind,
And those rich rewards are waiting for you.

I can't help but be a little selfish;
My anger is bursting out.
Your leaving is so unjust and unfair;
All I want to do is shout!
Please reconsider;
Do you have to go right now?
I'm just getting to know you better…
Perhaps an encore with a bow?

I know you have to leave today
And cast off your mortal shell,
But waking up tomorrow without you here
Will feel like a living hell!

Wish I Could Have Done More

You asked for nearly nothing
But some sweet kisses in return,
And yet you lay there suffering
While my face tears slowly burn.
The cancer now has ebbed your life,
There's nothing more we can do;
I wish I could take away all of your strife
And heal you through and through.
But now's the time you must move along
And leave me here to weep;
Let me just hold you one more time
As I lay you down to sleep.

Mischief

My heart went backwards in motion today,
When your soul swept with it my gladness away.

I want you to know the way you made me feel
And how much you helped my heart learn how to heal.

I'll never forget the feel of your fur;
You're with me forever, of that much I'm sure.

I'd like to send with you my support and love;
I'll miss you forever, my sprightly, sweet dove.

I Will Not Forget

I was blessed to know you,
To care for you until the end.
I was lucky to have you,
Not just as a pet, but as a friend.
I truly believe you knew me
Better than most people do.
I would confide in you the most;
You gave me courage to push through.
So I will be strong for you
Because I know that is what you would want.
I will hold you in my heart.
I will never forget you; indeed, I will not.

Face in the Clouds

The furnace was hot
Yet the ashes were cold
As we walked you from the lot.
Our teary eyes still mourned your loss;
Our hearts were so distraught.

Yet there upon the azure sky
A cloud rose up and formed
A likeness of your smiling face
And our hearts were quickly warmed.

Like some magical act that plays on high,
It put our grief at ease;
For there we saw your spirit shine
As it passed between the trees.

So now if we look so very close,
We can feel your presence there
And rest our minds in knowing that
You're with us everywhere.

Continued Healing

Embracing poetry is one way to help heal the pain from pet loss grief. We all need support when we have lost a pet and comfort can come in many different ways, depending on your personality and that of your beloved companion.

You may find solace participating in a support group, reading books on the subject, or engaging with the creative side of healing such as by spending time with this book.

Whatever way you choose to process your emotions, please be kind to yourself. Go through this powerful yet difficult journey without self-judgment, criticism, or intolerance for your process. Honor who you are and the life you had with your friend.

Everyone experiences loss differently and finding what works for you is part of the healing journey. You and your pet share or may have shared an incredible life together. These times are special occasions you will always treasure and hold deeply in your soul. There is an unspoken respect and confidentiality between the both of you to be cherished.

There are many emotions that accompany loss and I have found poetry is one way for people to feel the softer side of what they are experiencing. Grief can leave us feeling raw, angry, sad, depressed, etc. You can expect to have these feelings and know you are not alone. But it is also nice to have respite and feel the gentleness of grief, too.

A poem can be extremely beneficial and healing. Poetry has a way of soothing your soul, an uncanny power to heal your heart, when you have experienced sudden, unexpected pet loss.

A poem can offer a kind and loving way to rescue your heart as you recall memories of your pet in an inspired way. It is another instrument to allow joy to filter back in.

When you are ready, pet loss poems invite you to celebrate the special memories that you shared with your pet. They will give you inspiration and accountability to develop a different type of connection with your beloved friend that will last your lifetime.

Even though they may bring tears to your eyes, my hope is that, at the same time, they will rescue the joy you once felt with your beloved companion.

I hope you were able to find comfort and support while reading these poems, as I did when writing them. Each poem contains a special message to help you find hope, healing, and inspiration, for you do not need to walk your pet loss grief journey alone.

Warmly,

Wendy Van de Poll
August 1, 2018

How to Order Your Personalized Pet Loss Poem

Pet loss poems are a wonderful way to pay tribute and celebrate the life of your beloved companion. They can help with your grief when your pet is in pet hospice or when they have reached the end of their life.

Any time pet loss grief is present, poems can help heal your heart and soul.

If you would like to order one for yourself, please go to **https://centerforpetlossgrief.com/personalized-pet-loss-poem.** There you will find easy instructions to follow to order your special poem.

Resources

Center for Pet Loss Grief, LLC

Center for Pet Loss Grief.com
www.centerforpetlossgrief.com

Personalized Pet Loss Poems
www.centerforpetlossgrief.com/personalized-pet-loss-
poems

Online Support

Facebook
https://facebook.com/centerforpetlossgrief

Pet Memorial Support Group
https://facebook.com/group/petmemorials.centerforpetl
ossgrief

Veterinarians

Veterinary Medical Association
http://ahvma.org

American Holistic Veterinary Medical Association
https://ahvma.org

Support Groups

Association for Pet Loss and Bereavement
https://aplb.org

Association for Human-Animal Bond Veterinarians
https://aahabv.org

Acknowledgments

I would like to thank all my clients who have trusted me to hear and share their stories of grief and celebration. These remarkable stories inspired me to write these poems.

I appreciate all my teachers of the fur, feather, and fin variety who continue to demonstrate great patience, respect, and compassion as I share their verse from the heart to paper.

A huge hug goes to my husband, Rick. He is a remarkable poet and human being who dedicates his life to the animals and the environment. He inspires my soul. You can find his books on Amazon, as well.

About the Author

As a pioneering leader in the field of pet grief support, **Wendy Van de Poll** is the founder of the Center for Pet Loss Grief. She is an international bestselling author who provides wisdom, joy, compassion, and tools for grief relief through live and online events, tele-seminars, webinars, and/or radio shows. Wendy's presentations inspire, educate, and change the lives of her listeners.

In her practice, Wendy provides a safe place for dedicated pet parents and pet professionals who want support and guidance with pet loss grief, hospice for pets, and coping with the loss of their pets.

Wendy is dedicated to providing a calm place for her clients to express their grief over the loss of their pets. She does not tell them what to do but allows her clients to learn and approach their journeys with her empathetic guidance.

Her passion to help people when they are grieving over the loss of a pet and her larger-than-life love for animals have led her to devote her life to the mission of increasing the quality of life between animals and people, no matter their stage in the cycle of life.

What makes Wendy successful with her clients is that she gets grief. Because of her own personal experiences navigating the pet grief journey as well as her vast experience coaching others through grief and then finding JOY again after the death of their pets, she has become a sought-after end-of-life coach for pets and their people.

Wendy is a certified end-of-life and grief coach and a tested animal communicator and medium. She is also a certified pet funeral celebrant. She holds a Master of Science degree in wolf ecology and behavior and has run with wild wolves in Minnesota, coyotes in Massachusetts, and foxes in her backyard.

Wendy also coaches people who want to self-publish their own books about their pets and other topics.

You can reach her at:

www.centerforpetlossgriefcom/contact.

Thank You for Reading

Pet Loss Poems:
To Heal Your Heart and Soul

As the author of this book, I appreciate you buying and reading it. I hope you found the poems comforting for healing your heart and soul as you journey through pet loss grief.

I would be grateful if you would leave a helpful book review, either with your favorite book distributor or with Amazon.

Thank you,

Wendy Van de Poll, MS, CEOL

Bestselling Author, Speaker, Certified End-of-Life and Pet Loss Grief Coach

Founder of the Center for Pet Loss Grief, LLC.

www.centerforpetlossgrief.com

www.wendyvandepoll.com

For all of Wendy Van de Poll's books, please visit:

https://www.amazon.com/Wendy-Van-de-
    Poll/e/B01BMUWX7O.

Bestselling and Award-Winning Books
By Wendy Van de Poll, MS, CEOL

Pet Bereavement Series

My Dog Is Dying: What Do I Do?
My Dog Has Died: What Do I Do?

My Cat Is Dying: What Do I Do?
My Cat Has Died: What Do I Do?

Healing a Child's Pet Loss Grief

The Pet Professional's Guide to Pet Loss

Human-Animal Books

*Animal Wisdom: Conversations From The Heart
Between Animals and Their People*

Free Book

Healing Your Heart From Pet Loss Grief

Children's Picture Books

The Adventures of Ms. Addie Pants Series
The Rescue
The Ice Storm
New Friends
Off to School

To receive notification when more books are published, please go to:

https://centrforpetlossgrief.com
or
https://wendyvandepoll.com.

We will add you to the mailing list after you download your free gift.

Made in the USA
Las Vegas, NV
27 October 2024

10541155R00049